Introduction

This book introduces another unique c
based on an idea by Jill Walters of Tas
delicate flower-like shapes which can b
There are eight other delightful flowers
presented in Pat Ashby's inimitably ea
ingenious applique work by Diana Bees

G000152599

There are two brilliantly simple ideas ~~by Pat Trunkfield for the~~ varicut
cutter, the subject of Book 10.

Templates of the other cutters referred to in the book are shown on Pages
37 to 39.

The Tools. General Notes: Non-stick. One of their most useful aspects is
their non-stick property, which is inherent in the design and material used.
It is not a surface finish and, therefore, cannot wear off. It also means they
cut cleanly, without fuzzy edges.

Materials. All the tools can be used with any soft material such as
flowerpaste, sugarpaste, Permapaste, marzipan , modelling chocolate,
plasticine, modelling clay, etc.

Temperature. Normally hand washing in warm soapy water is all that is
required. They will withstand boiling water or the dishwasher without
deforming.

Handles. All the cutters have handles or fit comfortably into your hand,
which allows you to exert firm pressure over the whole of the cutting
edges.

Stability. They will not rust, corrode, deform or wear out with normal
useage. They should **NOT** be 'scrubbed' on the board or twisted.

Marking. All the tools are permanently marked to aid easy identification.
Metal. The cutters are delicate and should not be brought into contact with
sharp metal objects which may damage the cutting edges or surfaces. i.e.
keep them separated from metal cutters.

Hygiene. The materials meet the appropriate EEC regulations for food
hygiene.

Endorsement. All the items are personally endorsed and used by PAT
ASHBY, our Technical Director, who is one of the leading teachers of
sugarcraft in the UK and is an International judge, author and demonstrator.

1

THE NEW CUTTERS *(See Illustration 1)*
(Full size cut-out shapes are shown in Illustrations 2 and 3).
The Lace Flower Set (LF1, LF2, LF3, LF4)
This unique set of cutters can make delicate flower-like decorations, or side and corner pieces. They can be used to make ethereal looking collars or cradles. Because the effect is created by one press of the cutter, it is very easy for anyone to try out their skills. The results are only limited by your imagination!
The Extra Large Calyxes (R11D, R11E, R11F)
These three extend the range of our existing calyxes from 19mm (_") to 104mm (4") all with the same basic delicate shape. The four larger ones complement the Lace flowers and can be used to give contra-coloured effects.
Only the cutout shape of R11D is shown, which is exactly the same size as the outer shape of LF3. R11E and R11F are exactly the same size as the outer shapes of LF2 and LF1 respectively.

How to make the Lace Flower *(See Illustration 4).*
1. Roll out White flowerpaste and cut out 2 – LF1, by pressing the cutter firmly into the paste and running your fingers over the petals. Do not scrub or twist. Remove the inside cutouts. Leave one to dry more or less flat. Prop up the tips a little with Cloud drift
Cut out 2 – LF2 and glue into the centre of the second LF1 with rose water, but interleaving the sepals. Prop up into a cup shape with Cloud drift. Leave to dry.
2. When dry, glue onto the centre of the first LF1, interleaving as before. Leave to dry.
3. Paint or dust the tips of the petals with Orchard Rubine or Carmine. If desired a candle may be stuck into the centre with Royal Icing or paste glue. OR
4. Keep the inside cutouts, ball and cup them. Add to the centre of the flower with about a dozen stamens. (See Illustration 5).

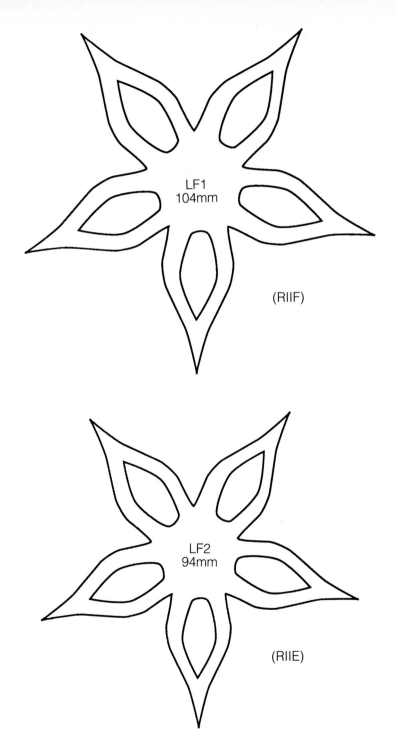

LF1
104mm

(RIIF)

LF2
94mm

(RIIE)

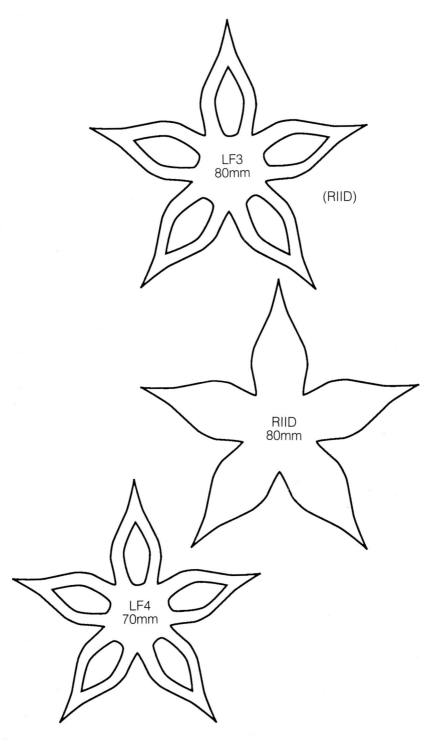

LF3
80mm

(RIID)

RIID
80mm

LF4
70mm

4

5

6

How to make the Flame Flower (*See Illustration 6*).

1. Centre. Hook a 26 gauge wire and glue a small sausage of paste on the end. Make 6 altogether. Leave to dry.

2. Roll out White flowerpaste and cut out 1 – LF2. Remove the inside cutouts. Glue the sausage of paste and thread a wire through the centre of the petal. Twist the petals up and press round the base of the flower to ensure good adhesion to the sausage. Bend the tips inwards a little. Hang upsidedown to dry. Dust the base Green, shading to Yellow Glo with Rubine tips. Steam.

3. Repeat Step 2 for buds as required.

4. Petals. Roll out White flowerpaste and cut out 1 – LF2 petal. Remove the inside cutouts. Cut across the centre to leave 3 sepals only. (See Illustration 7). Place the top of another wire in the centre of the base of the 3 sepals, glue, twist and fold over the righthand sepal to trap the wire at its base. Apply a little glue at this point and fold over the lefthand sepal in the same way. Make sure the wire is securely attached. Leave to dry.

5. Repeat Step 4 four more times. Dust the base Rubine shading into Yellow Glo with Orchid Mauve/Rubine tips. Bend the wire so that the petal assumes a nearly horizontal position.

6. Leaves. Hook a 33 gauge wire and glue a tiny ball of paste onto the hook. Make 15 altogether. Leave to dry.

7. Roll out Green flowerpaste and cut out 3 – LF3. Remove the inside cutouts. Cut each one into 5 individual sepals. Glue a wired ball from Step 5 into the centre of the base of a sepal. Squeeze around the base – curve and leave to dry. Repeat for the remaining sepals/wires. (See Illustration 8).

8. Assembly of Flower. Tape 3 petals together – then tape the remaining 2 in between. Thread the centrewire from Step 2 through the centre of the petals. Then tape on the leaves as required.

9

How to make the Lace Cradle (*See Illustration 9*).

1. Make a tiny baby in flowerpaste. Roll out White flowerpaste and cut out one rose petal R2. Frill around the outside with the frilling tool. Wrap around the baby. Leave to dry. Colour to choice.

2. Roll out White flowerpaste and cut out 2 – LF3, by pressing the cutter firmly into the paste and running your fingers over the petals. Do not scrub or twist. 'Glue' the centre with rose water and press the second petal on top of the first but interleaving the sepals. Place into a petal former or apple tray. Leave to dry.

3. Repeat Step 2 with LF4.

4. When dry, turn the LF3 pieces upsidedown and glue the LF4 pieces on top.

5. Sunshade. Roll out White flowerpaste and cut out one LF4 and leave to dry in an apple tray.

6. Hook a 26 gauge wire and glue a small ball of paste on the hook. Push into the centre of the LF4 piece and leave to dry. When dry, bend the wire to shape.

7. Glue a ball of paste to the other end of the wire and press underneath the centre of the base petals from Step 4. Finish with a blossom (F2L) in the centre top of the sunshade. Dust the edges with colour of choice.

10

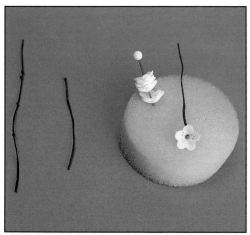

11

12

13

Template
14

How to make the Phlox. (See Illustrations 10 & 13).

1. Flower. Make a Mexican Hat using the second smallest hole in the Mexican Hat Adaptor (M1) and roll out from the centre. Pop the primrose cutter over the top (F3M) and cut out one flower. Place on the Orchard 'Paddy' (PDH) and soften the edges with the balling tool OP1. Make a small hole in the centre using the pointed end of the veining tool OP2. Thread a hooked 28 gauge wire through the centre, and roll the back of the flower between finger and thumb to make a long slender back.

Glue a Yellow stamen into the centre. Leave to dry. (See Illustrations 12 & 13).

2. Centre of flower. Around the centre at the bottom of each petal paint a fat 'V' in Burgundy. Lightly stroke Pink lines up from the V of each petal. Turn over and paint Pink lines on the back of each petal.

3. Calyx. Roll out Green flowerpaste and cut out one calyx (R15). Soften the edges, thread up the wire and press around the bottom of the flower.

4. Bud. Hook a 33 gauge wire and attach a tiny sausage of White paste, pointed at both ends. Make 5 grooves along the length. Leave to dry. When dry paint the grooves Green.

5. Leaves. Cut from Green florists tape and tape down the wire. Paint the stem Burgundy. See Template 14.

14

How to make the Spiraea Canescens (*See Illustrations 10 & 14*).

This is a deciduous shrub with small heads of white flowers, which are borne in profusion. Clusters of six down a brown stem.

1. Flower. Roll out White flowerpaste and cut out several blossoms using F2S and F2M cutters. Soften the outside of the petals with the balling tool OP1. Push a dressmakers pin through the centre and thread them up. Hold the end of the pin and flick the pin with your finger to separate the flowers. Stick into your pad until you are ready. The flowers are almost flat. (See Illustration 11).

2. Centre. Tie a single knot in a 33 gauge Green wire, and repeat along the wire every 1" (2cm) or so. Mash down some Rose Green paste with water for glue. Cut the wire just above a knot and dip the knot into the 'glue'. Thread the wire through the centre of the flower, pushing the flower up the wire to fit snugly round the centre. Leave to dry.

3. When dry, paint a Yellow circle around the Green centre. Paint 3 tiny Rose Green spots in a triangle on each petal with a 000 paintbrush. A tiny Green calyx can be painted on the back, but, as it cannot be seen, it seems to be unnecessary work.

4. The flowers are taped in clusters of 6. Tape the clusters, approximately $^3/_4$" from the flower, onto a 24 gauge Brown wire.

15

16

How to make the Frittelaria Meleagris – Snakes Head

(See Illustration 15).

1. Centre. Tape a small piece of narrow florists tape to the end of a 28 gauge wire, allowing it to protrude over the end. Cut into 3 and flatten out into a propellor shape. Tape 6 Yellow stamens around the base of the pistil, the top approximately halfway up the petal.

2. Flower. Push a piece of White flowerpaste into the smallest hole on the Mexican Hat Adaptor (M1), roll out the brim and cut out a six-petal flower N1.

Widen each petal with the 'Slimpin'. Move to the Orchard pad PD1 and soften the edge of the petals with the balling tool OP1. (See Illustration 16). Pinch a vein down the centre of each petal with tweezers. Turn the flower over and mark a vein down the centre of each petal with the pointed end of the petal veining tool OP2. Ball each petal from the tip to the centre to curl them up.

Put a little paste at the base of the stamens and thread the wire through the centre of the flower. Squeeze the base of the flower gently to make sure the centre is attached. Leave to dry.

3. Paint 6 Lime Green and a few Burgundy/Orchid Mauve stripes in the centre of the flower, radiating outwards. From the end of these stripes, paint a chequered pattern on the inside of all the petals with Burgundy/Orchid Mauve using a 000 paint brush. (See Illustration 17).

On the outside of the flower, paint the base of the petals Lime Green and paint a Burgundy/Orchid Mauve stripe in the centre of each petal, from the base.halfway up. Paint the chequered pattern on the outside of all the petals with Burgundy/Orchid Mauve using a 000 paint brush.

4. Small bud. (See Illustration 16). Make a small cone of Lime Green paste on the end of a 28 gauge wire and taper both ends. Mark 6 grooves round the bud. Dust Dark Green. Paint Dark Burgundy marks in the grooves.

5. Large bud. Make a cone of Pale Lime Green paste on the end of a 28 gauge wire. Dust the top a darker Green. Paint 6 – Burgundy stripes down the length of the bud. Paint the chequered pattern on the remainder of the bud.

6. Leaves. Glue a small sausage of Light Green paste onto the end of a 33 gauge wire. Press out with your fingers on either side of the wire to flatten it. Roll out each side with the Slimpin. Cut round the paste to produce a long slender leaf with a pointed end about $2^{1}/_{2}$" (6cm) long.

7. Place on the Orchard Pad (PD1) and gently ball round the edges. Mark a central vein with the pointed end of the veining tool (OP2). Curve to shape and leave to dry. When assembling the flower, the leaves alternate with the flowers down the stem.

17

18

19

How to make the Japanese Tree Peony. (*See Illustration 19*).

Centre.

1. Pop a ball of Burgundy flowerpaste onto the glued end of a 24 gauge wire and roll between your finger and thumb to elongate, and bring the end over the top end of the wire. Flatten the top and make 5 cuts with a knife. Twist the top of the pistil and leave to dry.

2. Tape about 60 Yellow long headed stamens round the pistil.

Flower. (See Illustrations 18 & 21).

1. Rub a little fat onto the board to prevent the paste from drying out too soon.

Roll out Burgundy coloured flowerpaste a little thicker than usual, and cut out 5 – Rose petals (R1).

2. Elongate the first petal by rolling with the rolling pin. Make a jagged edge round the top half by pressing hard and sliding off with the pointed end of the petal veining tool (OP2). (See Illustration 22).

3. Place on the Orchard Pad (PD1) and vein the petal by rolling the petal veining tool (OP2) over the surface. Soften the edges with the balling tool (OP1).

4. Place on a soft sponge and ball in the centre to cup it slightly.

5. Place in a flower former (approx. $2^1/_2$" dia.) or foil to dry.

6. Continue with the remaining petals in the same way, interleaving and glueing them in Step 5 to form a circle. Tuck the last petal under the first, propping with 'Cloud drift'.

7. Cut out a second row of 5 petals following Steps 1 to 4.

8. Place and glue them inside the first row with the middle of the first petal over a join in the first row.

9. Repeat Steps 1 to 6 with 5 – R2 petals, glueing them inside the second row. (See Illustration 22).

10. Thread the centre wire through the middle of the flower with a little glue and leave to firm. (See Illustration 23).

11. When firm, turn upside down.

12. Cut out 5 – more Burgundy petals with the 'Varicut' cutter set to A/C6/D1 (See Page 37), and proceed as Steps 2 to 4. (See Illustration 24).

13. Set and glue the first 'Varicut' petal on top of the first row of petals with the middle of the first petal over a join in the first row. Repeat for the remaining 'Varicut' petals, overlapping as before, and propping with 'Cloud drift'.

14. Turn flower over to adjust all the petals into the best positions and then turn upside down to dry. When dry, dust with Orchard Burgundy petal dust and steam. Paint the tips of the stamens with Burgundy.

Calyx.

1. Roll out Green flowerpaste and cut out one calyx R11C. Widen each sepal with the Slimpin.

2. Move to the Orchard Pad and soften the edges with the balling tool (OP1). Mark a centre vein down each sepal with the pointed end of the petal veining tool (OP2).

3. Glue the base of the flower and slide the calyx up the wire underneath the flower and press gently into position.

Template
20

4. Tape two more 24 gauge wires onto the stem. This strengthens the stem, since it is a very heavy flower.

Leaves.

1. Side leaves. Roll out a sausage of Green flowerpaste onto the grooved board and cut out 2 leaves with the 'Varicut' set at A/C3/D1. Vein with a dry leaf or suitable veiner.

2. Top leaves. Glue a ball of Green flowerpaste onto the end of a 24 gauge wire. Roll between your fingers to stretch it down the wire. Press either side of the wire with your fingers. Lay on a board and roll from the centre out each side with the Slimpin. Cut round the edge to fashion the three segments following the Template 20.

3. Vein and soften the edges with the balling tool OP1. Lay on a curved surface to dry thoroughly. (The centre segment of the three is the only one to have a wire) Dust the outside edges with Orchard Burgundy petal dust.

21

22

23

24

25

26

How to make the Clerodendrum Thomsoniae (*See Illustration 25*).

1. Bud. Prepare a small cone of Cream flowerpaste on the end of a 28 gauge wire. Roll out Cream flowerpaste and cut out one calyx R11A.

Vein each sepal with the Petal Veining Tool (OP2) and mark a centre vein.

Turn over onto a soft sponge and press in the centre with the balling tool (OP1) to cup.

2. 'Glue' the cone and thread the wire through the centre of the flower. 'Glue' both inside edges of each sepal and pinch the sides together firmly, continuing down to the point. Continue until all five sepals are firmly glued together. (See Illustration 26).

3. Flower. Tape 5 Lime Green stamens onto the end of a 30 gauge White wire. (On assembly these will protrude $3/4$" (2cm) from the flower). Curl the stamens by holding firmly and stroke the back of your scissors up the length of the stamens. Paint the tips of the stamens Orchard Burgundy.

4. Roll out Red flowerpaste and cut out 1 – Five petal flower (F10). Move to the pad and soften the edges with the balling tool (OP1).

5. Interleave the petals, glueing as you go, and press each petal firmly, leaving the last petal, thus creating a gap through which the stamens will protrude.

Pop onto a soft sponge and press in the centre with the balling tool (OP1) to cup.

6. 'Glue' the base of the stamens and thread the wire through the centre of the flower. Squeeze the base. The stamens should curl away through the gap in the petals. Leave to dry in the flower stand.

7. Roll out Cream flowerpaste and cut out one calyx R11A.

Vein each sepal with the Petal Veining Tool (OP2) and mark a centre vein.

Turn over onto a soft sponge and press in the centre with the balling tool (OP1) to cup.

8. 'Glue' both inside edges of each sepal and pinch the sides together firmly, up to halfway to the point. 'Glue' the base of the Red flower and thread through the centre until the points curl neatly under the flower. Glue some of the points of the sepals to the back of the flower. Pinch the edges of the sepals together a little further.

9. Finish with a tiny ball of Lime Green paste glued and threaded up the wire to tuck neatly at the base of the flower.

27

How to make the Clerodendrum Nutans (See Illustration 27). (Based on an idea by Beryl Baker – N.S.W.)

General. A beautiful shrub with long hanging sprays of white flowers against glossy dark green foliage.. Leaves vary considerably in size and the small ones have one central vein only. Medium and larger leaves have side veins also. Late autumn to winter flowering. Grows to approx. 1½ metres in part shade in Australia.

1. Centre. Cut off one end of fine White stamens (5 per flower), leaving the stamens as long as possible. Colour the tips with Brown liquid food colour. Bend over finger or pencil to give a graceful curve. Tape to 33 gauge Green wire and leave to dry. (See Illustration 28).

2. Buds. Make about 8 or 10 long round tipped buds for each spray in various sizes using White flowerpaste. Mark 5 fine grooves in each about $^2/_3$ length of the bud. Dust base with Pale Lime Green.

3. Flowers. Make a Mexican Hat with White flowerpaste and cut out 1 – N4 six petal flower. Cut off one petal and the tips of the remaining petals.

4. Roll the Petal Veining Tool (OP2) from side to side lengthwise on each petal to widen them out slightly and to vein them. Soften the edges with the balling tool (OP1).

5. Hollow out the centre of the flower with OP2 and gently curve back the petals slightly, leaving a gap where the sixth petal was removed.

6. Petal dust the throat and base of the flower with Lime Green.

7. Insert the 5 wired stamens – most of these curve out over the petals but not all. Leave to dry.

8. Repeat Steps 3 to 7 five times for each spray.

9. Calyx. Roll out Green flowerpaste and cut out 1 – R13 Calyx. Snip off the tip of each sepal. Vein the back of each sepal with one vein down the centre(OP2).

10. Ball the centre of the calyx on soft sponge to cup it, apply a little rose water to the centre and thread onto the stem of the flower. Press gently onto the underside of the flower to stick and bend the sepals back a little from the flower.

11. Dust the outside of the calyx with Rubine and Orange randomly, allowing some Green to show through here and there.

12. Repeat Steps 9 to 11 for each flower.

Template 27A

28

29

13. Repeat Steps 9 to 11 for each of the buds using the smaller calyx cutters R13A and R15, but cup the calyxes so that they almost close up leaving just enough room to insert the buds. For the slightly open calyxes dust the tips only on the outside. (See Illustration 29).

14. Leaves Place a ball of Dark Green flowerpaste onto a 33 gauge wire and roll out into a sausage shape. Then roll out each side of the wire with the Slimpin to flatten the paste out. Cut out various sized leaves wih the plastic knife following the general pattern of the largest one shown in Template 27A. The smallest leaves have only one vein down the centre.

15. Dust with Dark Green petal dust.

16. To give the shiny gloss, either 'steam' each leaf for a few seconds or apply edible varnish.

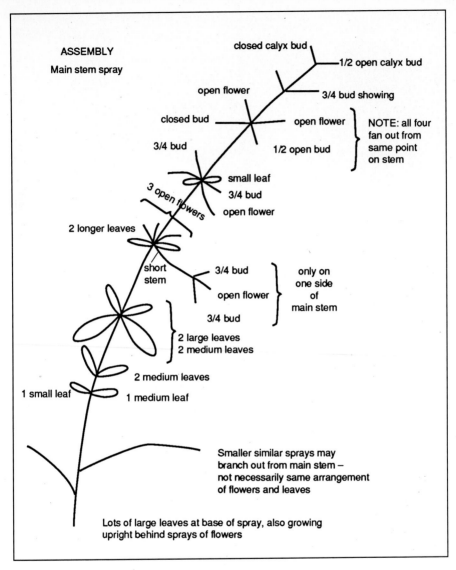

ASSEMBLY

Main stem spray

closed calyx bud

1/2 open calyx bud

open flower

3/4 bud showing

closed bud — open flower

3/4 bud — 1/2 open bud

NOTE: all four fan out from same point on stem

3 open flowers

small leaf

3/4 bud

open flower

2 longer leaves

short stem

3/4 bud

only on one side of main stem

open flower

3/4 bud

2 large leaves
2 medium leaves

2 medium leaves

1 small leaf

1 medium leaf

Smaller similar sprays may branch out from main stem – not necessarily same arrangement of flowers and leaves

Lots of large leaves at base of spray, also growing upright behind sprays of flowers

Diagram 30

17. Assembly. Flowers, buds and leaves usually appear in pairs (or fours) down a long main stem (26 gauge wire) – no leaves before the second and sometimes third set of buds/flowers as a rule. Leave a good space between each set on the stem ($\frac{1}{2}$" to $\frac{3}{4}$" on a real plant) and they are not necessarily the same arrangement on each side of the stem or spray. Smaller sprays can branch off the larger spray. (See Diagram 30).

The sprays hang down from a large mass of long Dark Green glossy leaves and would look lovely draped over the top edge of a cake.

31

How to make the Bluebells (*See Illustration 31*).

Buds. 1. Hook the end of a 30 gauge White wire. 'Glue' the hook and insert into a small ball of Violet flowerpaste. Roll between your finger and thumb to form a small sausage of paste with points a each end.

2. Make 5 vertical indentations round the bud. Dust the grooves with Orchard Violet. Paint the wire Dark Violet.

Flower.

3. Pistil and Stamens. Tape 1 stamen to the end of a 30 gauge wire and 5 smaller stamens around the pistil. Paint them Pale Violet with Green tips.

4. Roll out Violet flowerpaste thicker than usual and cut out 1 – Six petal flower (N5). Widen the petals on the board with the Slimpin.

5. Move to the Orchard Pad (PD1), vein each petal with the petal veining tool (OP2) and soften the edges with the balling tool (OP1). Mark a centre vein on each petal. (See Illustration 32).

6. Turn over and pinch a centre vein down each petal with tweezers. Turn back and ball from the tip of each petal to the centre with the balling tool.

Turn over onto a soft sponge and cup the centre.

7. Brush a little softened paste onto the base of the stamens and thread the wire into the flower. Pinch the tips. Hang upsidedown to dry.

8. Petal dust the veins and inside of the flower with a mixture of Orchard Violet and Midnight. Paint the stems the same colour.

9. For the main stem, tape 4 – 18 gauge wires together with Lime Green florists tape.

The flowers alternate down the stem.

10. Leaves. Glue a small sausage of Green paste onto the end of a 33 gauge wire. Press out with your fingers on either side of the wire to flatten it. Roll out each side with the Slimpin. Cut round the paste to produce a long slender leaf with a pointed end.

11. Place on the Orchard Pad (PD1) and gently ball round the edges. Mark a central vein with the pointed end of the veining tool (OP2). Curve to shape and leave to dry. Dust a Dark Green.

32

33

How to make the Star of Bethlehem (See Illustration 33).

1. Tape 6 Yellow stamens onto a 28 gauge wire.

2. Push a piece of White flowerpaste into the smallest hole on the Mexican Hat Adaptor (M1), roll out the brim and cut out 1 – Six petal flower (N4). Elongate each of the petals with the Slimpin.

3. Place on the Orchard Pad (PD1) and vein each petal with the petal veining tool (OP2). Mark a vein down the centre of each petal. Pop onto a soft sponge and cup in the centre with the balling tool (OP1).

4. 'Glue' the base of the stamens and thread the wire through the centre of the flower. Leave to dry. (See Illustration 34).

5. Paint a Lime Green streak on the back of each of the petals. The stems are Lime Green.

6. Bud. Hook a 28 gauge wire and glue a small ball of White flowerpaste onto the end. Leave to dry.

Roll out White flowerpaste and cut out 1 – Six petal flower (N4). Place on the Orchard Pad (PD1) and soften the edges with the balling tool (OP1). Mark a vein down the centre of each petal. Pop onto a soft sponge and cup in the centre with the balling tool (OP1).

7. 'Glue' the base of the ball and thread the wire through the centre of the flower, and cup the flower round the ball to create the bud. Leave to dry. When dry, paint a Lime Green streak down the centre of each petal.

8. Leaves. Glue a small sausage of Green paste onto the end of a 33 gauge wire. Press out with your fingers on either side of the wire to flatten it. Roll out each side with the Slimpin. Cut round the paste to produce a long slender leaf with a pointed end.

9. Place on the Orchard Pad (PD1) and gently ball round the edges. Mark a central vein with the pointed end of the veining tool (OP2). Curve to shape and leave to dry. Dust a Dark Green.

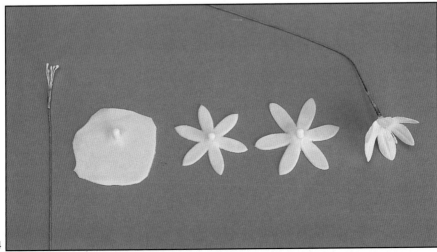

34

35

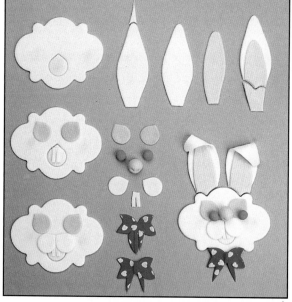

36

How to make the Rabbit Face (*See Illustration 35*) by Diana Beeson.

Note: The entire Rabbit face can be made up as you go, or cut out and dried, then put together later. If making as you go, glue with water or paste glue on to a plaque. If the pieces are dry, use Royal Icing. (See Illustration 36).

1. Face and Cheeks. Roll out White flowerpaste 'A' and cut out one P3 plaque. With the plaque lying horizontal, emboss a R4 Rose petal at the base of the centre curve (pointed tip of the petal upwards). Leave to dry. Cut out 2 – R4 Rose petals in White paste for the cheeks. Leave to dry.

2. Eyes. Roll out Grey flowerpaste and cut out 2 – R4 Rose petals. Roll 2 – small balls of Grey/Blue paste and position them slightly off centre on the Grey R4 petals. Flatten slightly and leave to dry.

3. Nose. Roll a piece of Pink paste the size of a large pea. Flatten slightly and insert the ends of pointed scissors into the base of the shape and cut. This gives the nostrils.

4. Teeth. Cut a tiny rectangle of White paste, then score down the centre lengthways, almost cutting in half. Separate at the cut end to form the teeth.

5. Ears. Roll out Grey paste and cut out 2 – ears with the 'Varicut' cutter set in A/C3/D1. Roll out Pink paste and cut 2 – inner ears with the cutter set in A/C2/D1. Round the tops of all the ears with the 'Varicut' tilted at a slight angle. Stick the Pink ears about 1/3rd of the way down the Grey ears.

Mark a line down the centre of both ears with the Petal Veining Tool OP2. Put the ears side by side, leaving a little gap between them, then position the P3 Plaque cutter horizontally across both of them, press down and cut away the base of the ears. The ears will now fit up against the P3 previously cut for the face, making it look as if the ears come from the back of the head.

6. Bow Tie. Roll out sugarpaste – coloured to choice, say Red – and cut out 1 – large Ivy leaf. Turn the leaf so that the long pointed end is facing you. With a Straight Edge Blade(LA2A) cut two lines halfway up the on either side of the centre. Bend the central strip thus formed backwards and tuck behind the curve of the top of the leaf. Make tiny cuts either side of the two remaining strips following the shape of the leaf. This will enable you to bend the two strips sideways and slightly under the leaf to form the ties of the bow. (N.B. Small heart shapes from the Lace Cutter Blade (LA2B) can be rolled into the surface of the sugarpaste before cutting out the Ivy leaf, to give a patterned bow tie).

37

37

How to make the Oriental Lady (*See Illustration 37*) by Diana Beeson.

1. Cover the cake and board with Champagne Regalice with extra Cornish Cream colouring and a touch of Skintone. Allow to dry for 24 hours.

2. Make a template the size of the top of the cake. Draw a line $1/4$" inside the edge all the way round. Place the template, covered by a sheet of waxed paper, on a board holding them both in position with masking tape.

3. Collar. Twist small balls of Red and Orange pastillage together. Roll out and cut out 2 – Japanese Maple Leaves (JM2). Vein lightly down each frond with the pointed end of the Petal Veining Tool (OP2). (Layer any excess paste from the rolling. Do not knead together – this keeps the colours marbled. Cover).

4. Following the template, lay the two leaves on the waxed paper, with the longest fronds just touching and the base of the leaves **not** over the inside line.

(N.B. As you follow the circle a slight adjustment will have to be made by bending the fronds so that they meet).

5. Roll out a little Green pastillage and cut out a smaller leaf (JM3) and vein as before. Moisten the back of the four fronds and place over the top and between the the two Red/Orange leaves. The centre point should just touch the fronds of the larger leaves. A small adjustment may be required.

6. Continue, adding one large leaf to either end of the collar, and then add the Green leaves in between, until both ends meet. This way, the pastillage will not dry out too quickly. Leave to dry.

Applique Lady. (See Illustration 38).

7. Face. Cut out a circle from thin White pastillage with GF2 and leave to dry.

8. Hair. Roll out Black sugarpaste, not too thinly. Roll the Petal Veining Tool (OP2) over the top of the paste in short strokes in one direction. This creates a lined effect for the hair. Cut out 2 – GF2 circles.

9. Take one of the circles with the lines North to South and cut off a $1/4$" segment at the base. Leave the segment on one side. Stick the cut circle onto the White dry circle from Step 7, with a little water, and smooth the edge of the hair to cover the edge of the circle.

10. The second Black circle is placed with the lines North to South and then cut in half North to South. Move the base ends of the two pieces about $3/4$" apart. Line up the GF2 cutter with the top edge and cut again. Remove excess paste.

Place these two pieces on either side of the first Black piece so that they leave a gap at the base of the head.

11. The Hairpiece. Using the segment from Step 9, cut a tiny V shape in the centre of the curved edge with the tip of a rose petal cutter R1. Place the resulting bow shape above the head and move the long ends upwards. The cut V opens and forms the right shape to sit on the head.

Decorate with three Red blossoms, cut with the blossom cutter F2S, piping a tiny dot of Royal Icing in the centre of each.

12. Eyes. Make eyes by cutting a teeny-weeny sausage of Black paste in half. Pick up with the pointed end of the veining tool, dip in water/glue and position on the face. Do the same with a tiny ball of Red paste for the mouth.

13. Bodice. Cut out 1 – rose petal (R1) from Red flowerpaste. Cut in half from tip to base.

With one half, straight edge away from you, fold the the left point over and down to the centre of the base of the shape. Then fold the right edge over the left side, leaving a gap in the middle, which forms the neck of the lady, and is in line with the lefthand fold.

Take the second half, placing it straight edge away from you as before. Place the first piece in the centre, slightly above the edge and fold as before, making another layer of the Kimono. Emboss with the pointed end of the petal veining tool (OP2) along the edges of the bodice.

14. The Dress. Roll out a larger piece of Red flowerpaste and with the Straight Blade (LA2A) of the Lace Cutter in holes 5, cut out a piece of lace $4^1/_2$ points long, with the half point on the left.

Emboss only with the Fan blade (LA2F), then turn the piece over. Fold the lefthand side over one pattern, matching the edge underneath, and now showing the embossed fan design. Fold the righthand side over one and a half patterns so that the half pattern overlaps the first fold, and all edges match. Emboss down the overlapping edge of the dress with the pointed end of the petal veining tool.

15. Sleeve. Roll out a larger piece of Red flowerpaste and with the Straight Blade (LA2A) of the Lace Cutter in holes 3, cut out a piece of lace $6^1/_2$ points long with the half point on the right. Emboss lightly with the Fan blade design (LA2F). Also emboss along each end of the sleeves with the pointed end of the veining tool. Turn the whole piece over.

16. Place the bodice in the centre of the sleeve about $^3/_4$" above the top straight edge. Then put the dress under the bodice, laying it at a slight angle. Fold over both left and right ends of the sleeves at an angle, so that both ends meet but do not overlap. Leave to dry.

17. With Orchard Majestic Gold dust and a little water, paint the embossed fan design on the dress and sleeves. Attach the Oriental Lady to the top of the cake with Royal Icing.

39

How to make the Christmas Card (*See Illustration 39*).

1. Roll out pastillage and cut out 3 – plaque shapes P1. Transfer to a dusted board and cut out the centre of one with the plaque cutter P3 to make a frame. Leave to dry.

2. While flat, decorate the edges and pipe *'Greetings'* with Royal Icing. Leave to dry. When dry stand the frame and one of the P1 plaques up on edge on top of the third P1 plaque 'glueing' into position with Royal Icing or paste glue. Prop with empty film containers until dry.

3. Roll out Green flowerpaste on the grooved board and cut out 9 holly leaves (H3 & H4). Glue the end of a 33 gauge wire and, holding the base of the holly leaf between your finger and thumb, gently insert the wire into the thick ridge. Vein the leaf with the leaf veiner R10.
Place on the Orchard Pad (PD1) and ball the edges with the balling tool (OP1) to make the leaf curl.

4. Roll out small balls of Red flowerpaste for the berries. Glue the end of a 33 gauge wire and insert into a berry. Paint a small Black spot in the centre of each berry.

5. Make a small quick rose as described in Book 5 Page 10 using Cutter F10.

6. Tape the small spray together and add a curl of Red paper ribbon. Arrange the spray so that the base of the 'stalk' is tucked inside the card. A small ball of sugar paste will make a firm base for the spray.

These cards can be used for all seasons.

40

How to make the Penguin (*See Illustrations 40 & 41*). by Pat Trunkfield

1. Roll out equal quantities of Black and White flowerpaste 'A' (or 50/50 Sugarpaste and flowerpaste).

2. Set the 'Varicut' Cutter to A/C6/D1 and cut out equal numbers of shapes in Black and White. Trim the base to a 'V' shape to create the tail. See Diagram 42.

Place a White shape on top of a Black shape. The further manipulation will stick them together.

3. Make two diagonal cuts in the sides for the wings as Diagram 42. and shape the wings as required.

4. Fold over the top to create the face, and pipe or paint in the eyes .

5. Fold in the two side panels and bend the tail underneath. It forms a 'S' shape. See Diagram 43.

6. Attach two small balls of Orange paste to the base as feet. Mark feet with two indentations for toes.

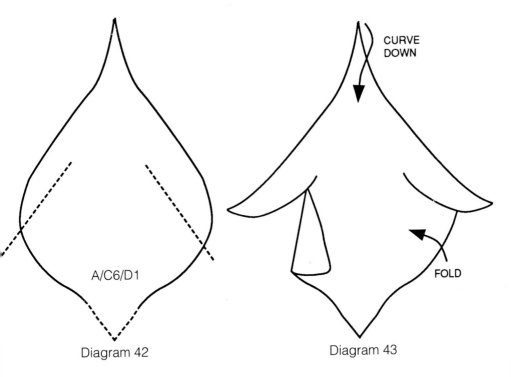

CURVE
DOWN

A/C6/D1

FOLD

Diagram 42

Diagram 43

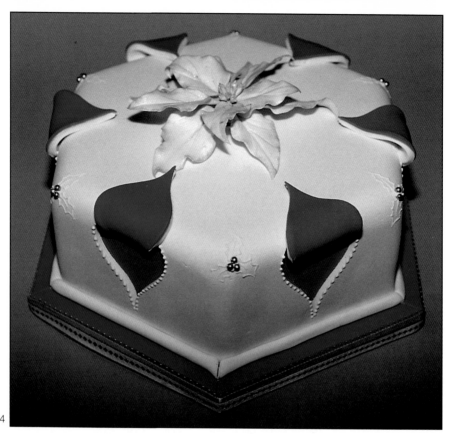

44

How to make the Cut-out Cake. (*See Illustration 44*). by Pat Trunkfield.

1. Cover a cake and separate cakeboard with a darker coloured sugarpaste – Blue or Red – and allow to harden.

2. Re-cover the cake with White sugarpaste, brushing the top and side corners with alcohol or boiled water to secure, and, while still soft, cut through the White paste only on the side, near the top, at regular intervals with the 'Varicut' cutter set to A/C6/D1. Curve the cutouts upwards onto the cake top.

3. Transfer the cake to the precoated board and trim the cake base with a simple straight roll of sugarpaste.

4. Roll out some more coloured paste – Blue or Red – and cut out some more A/C6/D1 shapes. Place a coloured shape over each White cutout and bend over the top. Soften some sugarpaste with water and pipe a small border round the side panels.

5. Repeat round the cake as required.

6. Pipe a three leaf holly design on each corner and use Silver dragees as berries.

7. Decorate the top with a simple poinsettia or lace flower.

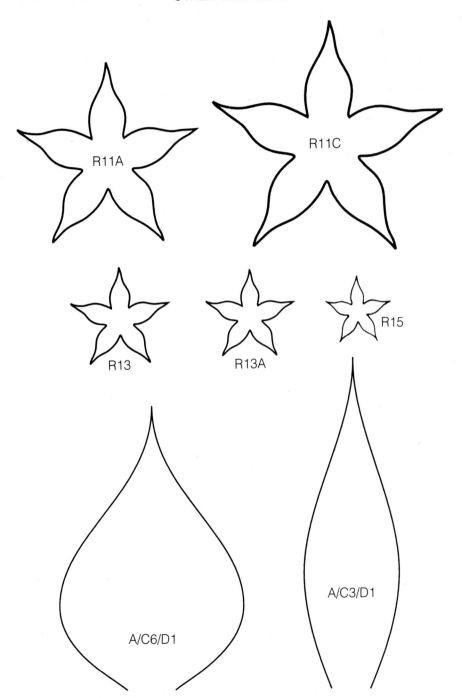

R11A

R11C

R13

R13A

R15

A/C6/D1

A/C3/D1

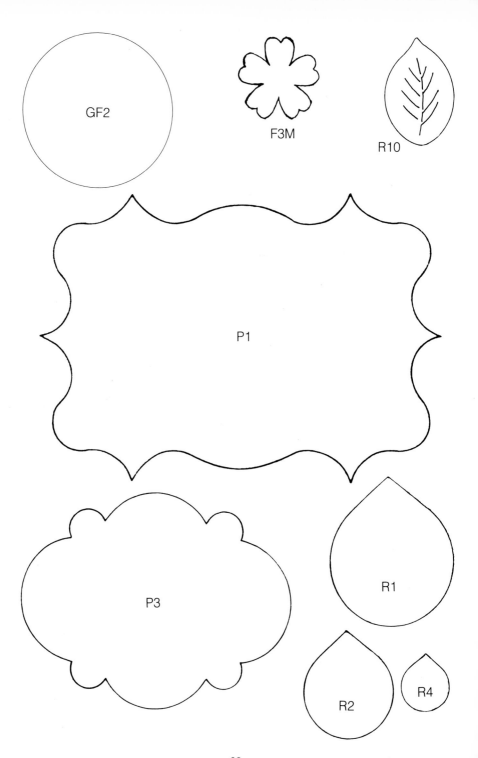

GF2

F3M

R10

P1

P3

R1

R2

R4

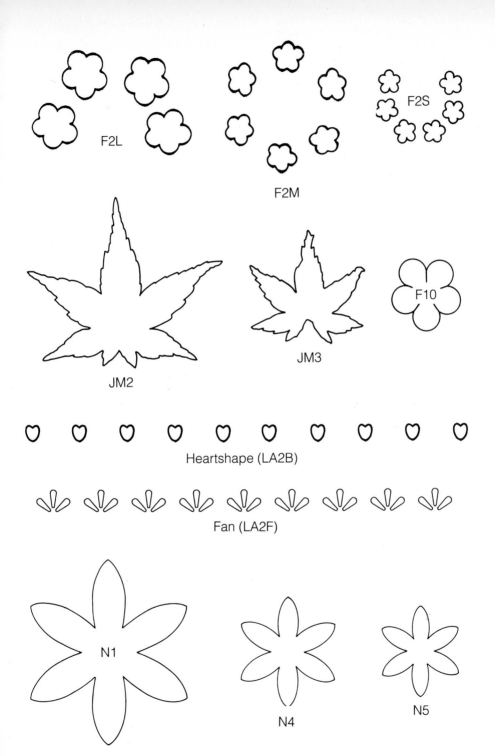

F2L

F2S

F2M

JM2

JM3

F10

Heartshape (LA2B)

Fan (LA2F)

N1

N4

N5

RECIPES

Flowerpaste A (or Lace Paste)

250g (½lb) Bakel's Pettinice or Craigmillar's Pastello **only.**

1 teaspoon (5ml) Gum Tragacanth

Rub 'Trex' on your hands and knead ingredients together until elastic. Wrap tightly in plastic cling film and store in an airtight container. Leave for 24 hours. Store in a cool place. This paste keeps well if worked through, say, once a week. Always keep tightly wrapped.

Flowerpaste D. 450g (1lb) sieved icing sugar
          5mls Gum Tragacanth and
          20mls CMC (Carboxymethylcellulose) – Tylose
          10mls white fat (Trex or Spry, not lard)
          10mls Liquid Glucose   *SOAKED IN 25MLS COLD WATER*
          45mls egg white   ℓ *10MLS POWDERED GELATINE*

Sieve all the icing sugar into a **greased*** (Trex) mixing bowl. Add the gums to the sugar. Warm the mixture in the microwave oven 3 x 50 secs on a medium setting, stirring in between.

Sprinkle the gelatine over the water in a cup and allow to 'sponge'.

Put the cup in hot, not boiling water, until clear. Add the white fat and glucose. Heat the dough hook beater, add the dissolved ingredients and the egg white to the warmed sugar, and beat on the lowest speed until all the ingredients are combined. At this stage the mixture will be a dingy beige colour. Turn the machine to maximum speed and mix until the mixture becomes white and stringy. Grease your hands and remove the paste from the machine. Pull and stretch the paste several times. Knead together and cut into 4 sections. Knead each section again and put into a plastic bag, then in an airtight container and keep in the refrigerator. Let it mature for 24 hours. This paste dries quickly so, when ready to use, cut off only a small piece and re-seal the remainder. Work it well with your fingers. It should 'click' between your fingers when ready to use. If it should be a little too hard and crumbly, add a little egg white and fat. The fat slows down the drying process and the egg white makes it more pliable.

Keep coloured paste in a separate container. This paste keeps for several months.

* This eases the strain on the machine considerably.

Pastillage C. Make up 8ozs Royal Icing. Add two level teaspoons Tylose. Mix thoroughly. Wrap in cling film and put into an airtight container. Leave 24 hrs before working.

Paste Glue.   1oz sugarpaste of the same colour as the item to be glued.
                 2 dessertspoons of warm water

Gradually combine together and place in the microwave oven for 1 – 1_ mins until the mixture boils. When cool use as required. Store at room temperature, or refrigerate if not to be used for a length of time. If the glue is to be used immediately then it is not necessary to boil it.